SPORTS GI___S
COLORING BOOK

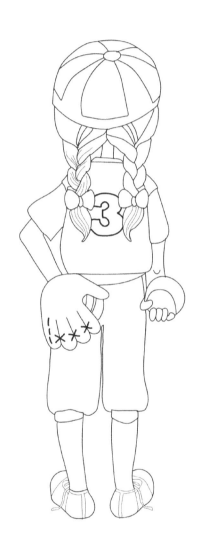

Cora Delmonico

We recommend using colored pencils, crayons, or gel pens for coloring. Markers are fine if you put a sheet of paper in between pages so it doesn't bleed though.

Tear this page out and use it between pages if you want to use markers.
You can use it over and over!

Made in the USA
Columbia, SC
07 April 2020